THIS IS
A BOOK FOR
PEOPLE
WHO LOVE

The
National
Parks

THIS IS
A BOOK FOR
PEOPLE
WHO LOVE

The
National
Parks

MATT GARCZYNSKI

ILLUSTRATIONS BY BRAINSTORM

RUNNING PRESS
PHILADELPHIA

Running Press
Hachette Book Group
1290 Avenue of the Americas, New York, NY 10104
www.runningpress.com
@Running_Press

Printed in China

First Edition: May 2020

Published by Running Press, an imprint of Perseus Books, LLC, a
subsidiary of Hachette Book Group, Inc. The Running Press name and
logo is a trademark of the Hachette Book Group.

The Hachette Speakers Bureau provides a wide range of authors for
speaking events. To find out more, go to www.hachettespeakersbureau.
com or call (866) 376-6591.

The publisher is not responsible for websites (or their content) that are
not owned by the publisher.

Text by Matt Garczynski.

Print book cover and interior design by Jenna McBride.

Library of Congress Control Number: 2019953019

ISBNs: 978-0-7624-6901-7 (hardcover), 978-0-7624-6902-4 (ebook)

RRD-S

10 9 8 7 6 5 4 3 2 1

CONTENTS

INTRODUCTION

BEGINNINGS

By the early twentieth century, most of California's redwood forest had been leveled by the lumber industry. The American bison, which once numbered in the tens of millions across the continent, had dwindled to under a thousand. In the Florida Everglades, the astonishing bird population had plummeted due to the pressures of the plume trade.

Yet these days, a different story can be told. Nearly half of California's remaining redwoods are preserved, with crews mobilized to replant entire hillsides in deliberate restoration efforts. American bison populations have increased twenty-five-fold, with most wild animals living within just a small handful of protected lands. The migratory

and year-round bird populations of the Everglades have slowly returned over the past several decades. While all around the world wild habitats succumb to profiteering, the areas within the national parks remain—with little exception—protected. From the vibrant canopy of Acadia's forests to the one-of-a-kind fauna of the Channel Islands, the parks offer wildly supportive places for diverse ecosystems to thrive.

How did this happen? The national parks movement owes its drive to the efforts of a persistent and visionary few, coming together at a crucial moment in American history. Among them, the gentle-eyed naturalist John Muir, who found his eventual cohort and patron in then-president Theodore Roosevelt. Writers like Ferdinand V. Hayden, John Wesley Powell, and Clarence King worked to raise public consciousness around the notion of protecting wilderness settings. The national parks idea helped to shift the popular narrative that the American frontier was strictly a grab bag for quick and easy wealth, an exciting game of "finders keepers" spurred by competition and greed. This sort of commerce came at the expense of vast expanses of wildlife and natural beauty, as well as countless indigenous lives.

At first, the parks were set aside as new kinds of wildlife zoos, whose locations and boundaries were  decided more for their spectacular scenery than out of consideration for their ecologies. However, as a new environmental consciousness arose over the years, the parks' incredible value as ecological preserves came to the fore. Today, a robust environmentalism lies at the heart of the National Park Service mission.

For roughly a century and a half, the national parks have offered a meaningful holdout against the shoveling of common lands into private control. The idea has sparked a global movement, with over 3,000 national parks popping up in nearly 100 different countries. Each year in the United States alone, national park sites welcome over 330 million visitors—a number commensurate with the entire population of the country.

THE WILDERNESS IDEA

The founding of the national parks, however, was not without its ironies. The effort to preserve American wilderness came in the wake of the Indian Wars, when the fledgling nation-state displaced vast numbers of people from their ancestral lands. In the process, the continent lost generations of traditional knowledge on how to care for its natural resources. And in its place, the modern cultural concept of "wilderness" sprang up to describe all places untouched, void of human existence, and thus, somehow, perfect. Many of the early tourists to locations such as Yosemite, Yellowstone, and Glacier

National Park came upon a romantic ideal of an America "before" human arrival, from which native populations had only recently been removed by attrition, shady dealings, and military force.

To many environmentalists, the idea of wilderness as a place where "man himself is a visitor who does not remain" (as defined by the 1964 Wilderness Act) is a troublesome one. It seems to distance humans from their responsibility to nature wherever they live and obscures the human role in shaping nature for worse or for better.

WHAT THE NATIONAL PARKS CAN TEACH US

Observing firsthand the magnificent sights of the national parks, we may take the opportunity to transform our own views on the natural world. We may even catch a glimpse of what John Muir saw, when he envisioned the whole globe as "one great dewdrop," the whole universe as "an infinite storm of beauty."

In profound ways, the national parks can open our eyes to a natural world that doesn't end at their borders. Being awed by stately herds of elk in Yellowstone, salmon runs up the cascades of Katmai, and the dazzling sandstone formations of Arches, we might be inspired to learn the names of plants, animals, and natural landmarks in our own neighborhoods. We might better notice the changing of the seasons, the appearance of the night sky above our homes, and the quality of the air we breathe. We might begin to bear witness to the effects of business, infrastructure, and our own consumption on the environment and feel called to action as John Muir and company were more than a century ago.

As the years ahead pose new challenges for the environment—in rising sea levels, temperatures, and atmospheric carbon levels—we can look to the example of the national parks in order to preserve, protest for, and restore our wild world. Humanity is what's known as a "keystone species," a member of the ecology on whom other species rely. The national parks offer a place to contemplate that role and achieve harmony with the planet that sustains us.

THIS IS A BOOK FOR PEOPLE WHO LOVE THE NATIONAL PARKS

PARK PROFILES

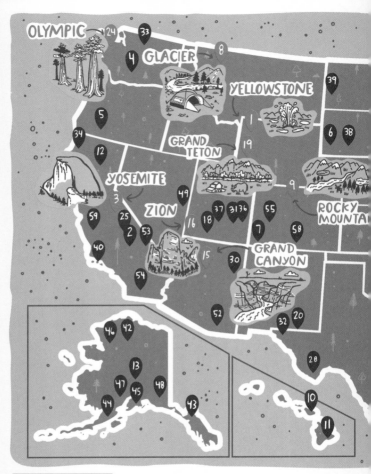

OLYMPIC 24 33

4 GLACIER 8

YELLOWSTONE 39

5

34

12

GRAND TETON

1

19

6 38

YOSEMITE

3

49

ZION

59 25

2 53

40

16 18

37 3136 55

7 58

9

ROCKY MOUNTAIN

54

15

30

GRAND CANYON

52

32 20

28

46 42

13

47 48

45

44

43

10

11

CANYONLANDS, UTAH
GUADALUPE MOUNTAINS, TEXAS
NORTH CASCADES, WASHINGTON
REDWOOD, CALIFORNIA
VOYAGEURS, MINNESOTA
ARCHES, UTAH
CAPITOL REEF, UTAH
BADLANDS, SOUTH DAKOTA
THEODORE ROOSEVELT, N. DAKOTA
CHANNEL ISLANDS, CALIFORNIA

41. BISCAYNE, FLORIDA
42. GATES OF THE ARCTIC, ALASKA
43. GLACIER BAY, ALASKA
44. KATMAI, ALASKA
45. KENAI FJORDS, ALASKA
46. KOBUK VALLEY, ALASKA
47. LAKE CLARK, ALASKA
48. WRANGELL-ST. ELIAS, ALASKA
49. GREAT BASIN, NEVADA
50. AMERICAN SAMOA,
    AMERICAN SAMOA

51. DRY TORTUGAS, FLORIDA
52. SAGUARO, ARIZONA
53. DEATH VALLEY, CALIFORNIA
54. JOSHUA TREE, CALIFORNIA
55. BLACK CANYON OF THE
    GUNNISON, COLORADO
56. CUYAHOGA VALLEY, OHIO
57. CONGAREE, SOUTH CAROLINA
58. GREAT SAND DUNES, COLORADO
59. PINNACLES, CALIFORNIA
60. GATEWAY ARCH, MISSOURI
61. INDIANA DUNES, INDIANA

ACADIA

LOCATED: Maine	ESTABLISHED: 1916
SIZE: 77 square miles	NATIVE PEOPLE: Wabanaki
SAMPLE WILDLIFE: Moose, white-tailed deer, harbor seal, puffin, bald eagle, peregrine falcon	

At the confluence of land and sea, evergreen and decid-uous, residential and "wild" lies Acadia National Park in coastal Maine, where visitors might wade through ankle-deep tide pools, go hiking in high glaciated peaks, or kick back in the comforts of a nearby resort town.

The park's densely wooded forests support a diverse array of evergreen spruces and firs, as well as colorful beeches, aspens, and sugar maples. Acadia's vegetative medley was ensured by the Fire of 1947, which laid waste many of the region's old-growth evergreens. This gave sun-loving species a chance to thrive, providing food for wildlife and even enhancing the scenery. The evergreens later returned, less uniformly dominant than before. The fire also reshaped the surrounding towns, driving the wealthy seasonal crowd out while permanent residents rebuilt their homes. Today, a row of motels stands in place of grand summer cottages, welcoming a wide range of visitors to the area.

Towering above Mount Desert Island is Cadillac Mountain, the highest point on the U.S.'s North Atlantic Seaboard. Early risers flock to its pink granite peak, to be the first in the country to see the sunrise.

AMERICAN SAMOA

LOCATED: American Samoa	ESTABLISHED: 1988
SIZE: 21 square miles	NATIVE PEOPLE: Samoan

SAMPLE WILDLIFE: Samoa flying fox, white-naped flying fox, Pacific sheath-tailed bat, Pacific slender-toed gecko, Pacific boa, wattled honeyeater

Encompassing the islands of Tutuila, Ta'ū, and Ofu, the National Park of American Samoa preserves the tropical plant life, marine ecologies, and native culture of the eastern Samoan islands. Working your way up the islands' volcanic peaks, you will notice gradual shifts between five rain forest communities: lowland, montane, coast, ridge, and cloud. Take in panoramic views of the majestic cliff-lined coasts from high up in the cloud forest of Lata Mountain.

The park sits on traditional communal land, which the National Park Service comanages with eight participating villages. Subsistence farming is permitted in the park, allowing for the perpetuation of *fa'asamoa*, the Samoan way of life. The word *Samoa* means "sacred center of the universe," pointing to the deep connection its people have to the land. While western Samoa achieved independence in 1962, the eastern islands remain under annexation by the United States. American Samoa is the only inhabited U.S. territory south of the equator.

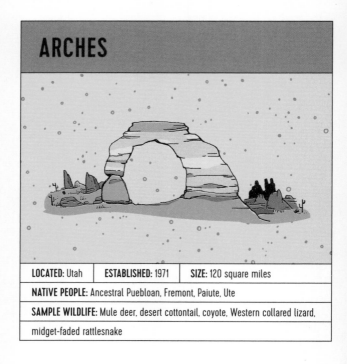

ARCHES

LOCATED: Utah	ESTABLISHED: 1971	SIZE: 120 square miles
NATIVE PEOPLE: Ancestral Puebloan, Fremont, Paiute, Ute		
SAMPLE WILDLIFE: Mule deer, desert cottontail, coyote, Western collared lizard, midget-faded rattlesnake		

The erosive forces of nature have sculpted this high-desert landscape into an orange-pink jumble of rock formations. Here you'll find the largest concentration of sandstone arches in the world, as well as pinnacles, spires, pedestals, and balanced rocks. Fins, the natural precursors to arches, jut up like the bony plates of the dinosaurs that once called this Utah desert home.

Devils Garden contains the most diverse array of rock formations in the park, with trails leading to various landmarks. The towering Landscape Arch, with an opening of 306 feet, is considered the longest natural stone span in North America. Farther south lies the rough-hewn terrain of the Fiery Furnace, a mess of vertical red slabs standing like sentinels in the rising sun. At their base, a labyrinth of narrow passages offers the perfect hike for thrill-seeking claustrophiles.

BADLANDS

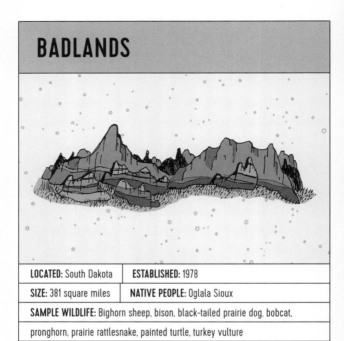

LOCATED: South Dakota	ESTABLISHED: 1978
SIZE: 381 square miles	NATIVE PEOPLE: Oglala Sioux
SAMPLE WILDLIFE: Bighorn sheep, bison, black-tailed prairie dog, bobcat,	
pronghorn, prairie rattlesnake, painted turtle, turkey vulture	

A strong wind howls through the canyon. The fossil of an ancient mammal emerges from the rainbow-striped stone. This is Badlands, named *maco sika* (*maco* = "land," *sika* = "bad") by the Lakota for its unforgiving weather and terrain. Reminders of a seafloor, lush tropical landscape, and open woodland are recorded in the sandstone. For over ten thousand years, the Badlands served as native hunting grounds. But that history came to a tragic close in the late nineteenth century, when homesteaders and U.S. troops forcibly drove tribes from the region. The South Unit of the park contains the site of one of the last known Ghost Dances, conducted as spiritual resistance to outside rule. Less than forty miles south of the park lies the historic site of the Wounded Knee massacre.

Beyond the buttes and canyons, the park contains the largest protected mixed-grass prairie in the National Park Service. These deeply rooted grasses coevolved with the once-massive herds of bison and nourish rich microbial ecosystems in the soil. Scientists have suggested that cultivating such grasslands could be an important tool in drawing excess carbon from the atmosphere and stemming the tide of climate change. In October 2019, the NPS reopened 22,000 acres of Badlands to grazing bison. "By ensuring that the largest of creatures are thriving," the National Park Foundation explained, "the park can more safely guarantee the health of the entire ecosystem."

BIG BEND

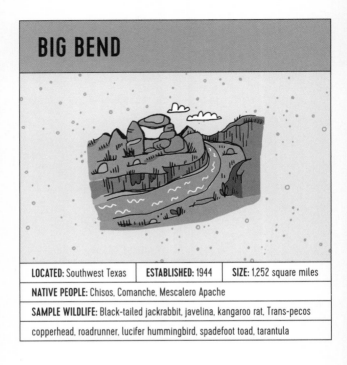

LOCATED: Southwest Texas	ESTABLISHED: 1944	SIZE: 1,252 square miles
NATIVE PEOPLE: Chisos, Comanche, Mescalero Apache		
SAMPLE WILDLIFE: Black-tailed jackrabbit, javelina, kangaroo rat, Trans-pecos		
copperhead, roadrunner, lucifer hummingbird, spadefoot toad, tarantula		

The stark shadows of the yucca sweep across the rippling sand, as the blazing sun cuts an arc across the wide West Texas sky. This is the Chihuahuan Desert, the largest desert in North America, which plays host to a sweeping oasis of beauty known as Big Bend National Park. Named for the broad meandering path carved by the Rio Grande river, the park is a refuge for more than 1,500 species of wildlife, including plants, insects, birds, reptiles, and mammals.

The park's climate is characterized by extremes—dry summer heat topping 100°F on the desert floor as well as the occasional subfreezing winter chills. Within the park lies the entire Chisos mountain range, where hikers will find a forest ecology that seems a world away from the desert below.

BISCAYNE

LOCATED: Florida Keys	ESTABLISHED: 1980
SIZE: 270 square miles	NATIVE PEOPLE: Creek, Glades culture, Tequesta
SAMPLE WILDLIFE: Manatee, American crocodile, brown basilisk, sea turtle, yellow-crowned night heron, pelican, lionfish, elkhorn coral	

Just off the shores of Miami, the Florida Keys begin their 125-mile arc west toward the Gulf of Mexico. This archipelago is home to Biscayne, one of the more unique parks in the U.S. To get to Biscayne National Park, you'll have to be willing to get a little wet—95 percent of the park is underwater. Dive down below the turquoise waves and observe colorful coral reefs teeming with life. Or paddle your way through a watery maze of mangrove forests on a sliver of lush green barrier islands.

As with many coastal parks, the threat of rising sea levels looms over the future of Biscayne. The ridge of reefs and mangroves serves as a hydraulic barrier keeping seawater from flooding the Everglades to the west. With ocean levels projected to rise thirty inches by 2100 that balance could be severely offset. The effort to preserve the national parks, especially those in coastal areas, is an effort to preserve the whole planet.

BLACK CANYON OF THE GUNNISON

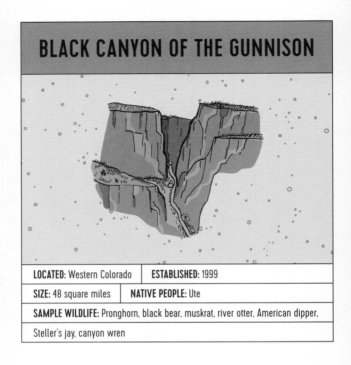

LOCATED: Western Colorado	ESTABLISHED: 1999
SIZE: 48 square miles	NATIVE PEOPLE: Ute

SAMPLE WILDLIFE: Pronghorn, black bear, muskrat, river otter, American dipper, Steller's jay, canyon wren

H. P. Lovecraft himself would have trembled at the sight of Black Canyon of the Gunnison, a steep, narrow gash in the Colorado wilderness. The canyon's 2,000-foot walls descend in cliffs and crags toward the shadowy Gunnison River below. Sculpting these walls took two million years of slow grinding work by the river and its tributaries, which run in narrow bands at their base. The name "Black Canyon of the Gunnison" (cue dramatic thunderclap) derives from its eerie black-stained walls, parts of which receive less than an hour's sunlight in a single day. Easy trails for visitors run on either side of the canyon's rim, while more strenuous hikes down waterworn ravines—unmarked and unmaintained—wind down to the very bottom.

BRYCE CANYON

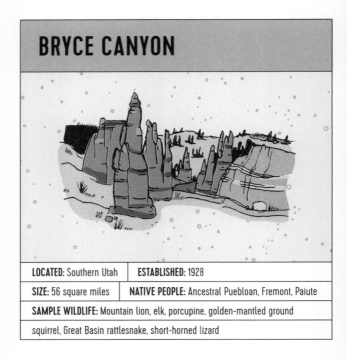

LOCATED: Southern Utah	ESTABLISHED: 1928
SIZE: 56 square miles	NATIVE PEOPLE: Ancestral Puebloan, Fremont, Paiute
SAMPLE WILDLIFE: Mountain lion, elk, porcupine, golden-mantled ground squirrel, Great Basin rattlesnake, short-horned lizard	

According to the Paiute, this place was once home to the Legend People, a mighty group who lived heavy off the bountiful rivers and pine nuts of the region. Leaving nothing for the other animals to survive on, they incurred the wrath of the trickster spirit Coyote, who turned them into pillars of stone. Their spindly forms still stand around Coyote's banquet table, a silent testament to their greed—and a reminder for generations to come.

These candy corn–like spires of Bryce Canyon are the hoodoos, ranging from 5 to 150 feet tall. Alternately pink, orange, red, and white, their colors seem to shift at different times of day. In the winter, their peaks are capped with fallen snow, adding to their otherworldly appearance.

Hikers along the rim of the canyon may stumble on the gnarly bristlecone pine, among the oldest living things on earth. These windblown patriarchs have made their roots in the dry desert soil for up to 1,600 years.

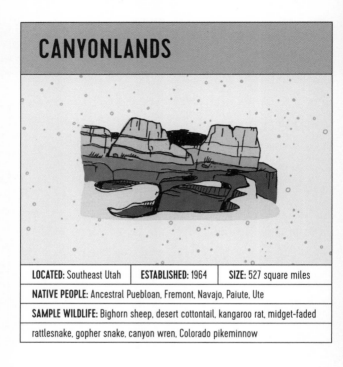

CANYONLANDS

LOCATED: Southeast Utah	ESTABLISHED: 1964	SIZE: 527 square miles
NATIVE PEOPLE: Ancestral Puebloan, Fremont, Navajo, Paiute, Ute		
SAMPLE WILDLIFE: Bighorn sheep, desert cottontail, kangaroo rat, midget-faded rattlesnake, gopher snake, canyon wren, Colorado pikeminnow		

The Colorado and Green Rivers converge at the base of a rocky labyrinth—the point at which they meet divides this park into four unique districts. The colorful landscape is rife with fins, arches, spires, buttes, mesas, and (of course) canyons in this panoply of geologic wonders. Driving between these districts can take up to six hours, since there are few places to cross the park from rim to rim. The most accessible, and most popular, district is the flat-topped mesa known as Island in the Sky, which offers panoramic views of the canyons, rivers, and far-off La Sal Mountains.

The Horseshoe Canyon was incorporated into the park in 1971 in order to preserve its cultural relics, including the Great Gallery. Artists of the Desert Archaic culture lined the sandstone walls of this canyon with silhouetted human figures who have stood watch over the landscape for centuries untold.

CAPITOL REEF

LOCATED: South-central Utah	ESTABLISHED: 1971
SIZE: 378 square miles	NATIVE PEOPLE: Fremont, Paiute, Ute
SAMPLE WILDLIFE: Pronghorn, mule deer, marmot, striped whipsnake,	
Great Basin spadefoot toad	

An upthrust fold in the earth extends a hundred miles across this red rock desert. White domes resembling stately capitol buildings jut up from along its crest, lending the park its name. Perhaps the least celebrated of Utah's "Mighty Five," a group that also includes Arches, Bryce Canyon, Canyonlands, and Zion, this playground of sandstone marvels is not to be overlooked.

Remnants of the region's cultural past are sprinkled throughout the park, from the Fremont petroglyphs etched into the rock face to the Gifford Homestead and historic orchard of the Fruita colony. The National Park Service maintains the orchard to this day, using old-school irrigation and cultivation techniques. From spring to early autumn, visitors can freely pick from harvests of cherries, apricots, peaches, pears, and apples.

The sky over Capitol Reef is a spotless window to the cosmos and one of the park's most precious resources. Park staff have carefully worked to prevent light pollution over the years, earning Capitol Reef its status as a Gold Tier International Dark Sky Park.

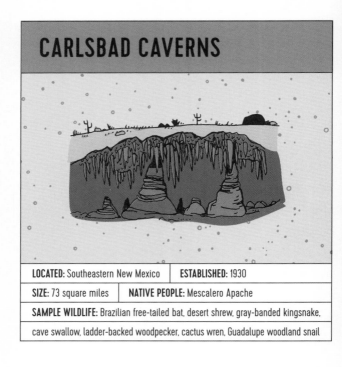

CARLSBAD CAVERNS

LOCATED: Southeastern New Mexico	**ESTABLISHED:** 1930
SIZE: 73 square miles	**NATIVE PEOPLE:** Mescalero Apache

SAMPLE WILDLIFE: Brazilian free-tailed bat, desert shrew, gray-banded kingsnake, cave swallow, ladder-backed woodpecker, cactus wren, Guadalupe woodland snail

This otherworldly network of caves was carved some four million years ago, in tandem with the Guadalupe Mountains. As the limestone uplifted, an "acid bath" of groundwater and hydrogen sulfide crept downward with the falling water table, leaving newly dissolved caverns in its wake. Some time later, a surface collapse created the present-day entrance, which welcomes nearly half a million visitors per year down into the caverns' honeycombing depths.

Easing the journey through this winding park is a 750-foot-long elevator ride, which renders optional the steep, more than mile-long hike into the enormous chamber known as the Big Room. Visitors have the option of trekking even farther along the Big Room Trail, enjoying such dazzling cave formations as stalactites, columns, soda straws, draperies, curtains, and ribbons. All told, the park is home to more than 119 known caves, including one of the deepest in North America. The 1,604-foot-deep Lechuguilla Cave is open only to research teams with special permission from the NPS.

Each summer at dusk, the cave's population of Brazilian free-tailed bats, numbering in the hundreds of thousands, spills out the mouth of the cave for an evening meal. Their dark fluttering wings fill the skies and bring an early nightfall to the desert below. An amphitheater outside provides the ideal viewing area for this eerie sight.

CHANNEL ISLANDS

LOCATED: Off the Southern California coast		**ESTABLISHED:** 1980
SIZE: 390 square miles	**NATIVE PEOPLE:** Chumash, Tongva	
SAMPLE WILDLIFE: California sea lion, island fox, island deer mouse, harvest mouse, spotted skunk, island night lizard, island scrub-jay, pelican, garibaldi, California spiny lobster		

A kelp forest sways with the cool Pacific tides, while schools of halfmoon fish weave their way through the leaves. Nearby on the slopes of Anacapa Island, brilliant yellow coreopsis blooms greet nesting California brown pelicans and western gulls. From beneath the blue waves to high up in the sky, the strikingly unique Channel Islands are abundant with plant and animal life.

Often called "California's Galápagos," this volcanic archipelago is home to nearly 150 plant and animal species found nowhere else on earth. The islands have sat isolated from the mainland since they were formed, but they've never been far. A twenty-mile boat or plane ride from Santa Barbara will get you there in no time. The 125,000 acres of submerged lands in the park provide a home for over 1,000 species of marine life. Kayakers and snorkelers can meet some of the waters' charismatic residents, such as the bottlenose dolphin or sea otters. Hikers will enjoy unforgettable views from a number of scenic trails and may observe the tens of thousands of seals and sea lions that rest along the islands' shores.

CONGAREE

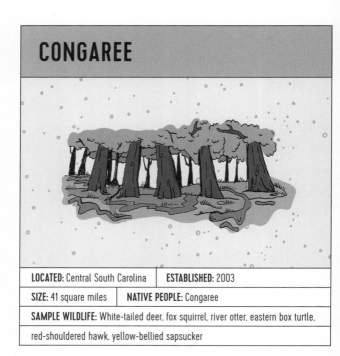

LOCATED: Central South Carolina	**ESTABLISHED:** 2003
SIZE: 41 square miles	**NATIVE PEOPLE:** Congaree

SAMPLE WILDLIFE: White-tailed deer, fox squirrel, river otter, eastern box turtle, red-shouldered hawk, yellow-bellied sapsucker

Every so often in this primeval hardwood forest, flood-waters from the Congaree River will sweep across the ground, turning the place into a swampy wonderland and bringing nutrients to the mucky soil. Year-round changes in the water level will form new streams, ponds, creeks, and puddles, creating new obstacles for hikers and new opportunities for canoers and kayakers.

While many of its trees may be centuries old, this forest remains dynamic and ever-changing.

Since its establishment as a National Monument in 1976, the Congaree forest has been preserved as the largest remaining tract of southern old-growth bottomland forest in the United States. Its trees are some of the tallest in the East, among them champion loblolly pine, sweetgum, cherrybark oak, and American elm. In this "Redwoods of the East," more than ninety different tree species can be found.

CRATER LAKE

LOCATED: Southern Oregon	**ESTABLISHED:** 1902
SIZE: 286 square miles	**NATIVE PEOPLE:** Klamath
SAMPLE WILDLIFE: Roosevelt elk, mule deer, black bear, pine marten, Townsend's chipmunk, golden-mantled ground squirrel, Clark's nutcracker, red-tailed hawk, Mazama newt, bull trout	

The ancestors of the Klamath who lived in this part of the Cascade Volcanic Arc around 7,700 years ago must have had their world rocked when Mount Mazama erupted and collapsed. What remained afterward was a bowl-like depression in the earth, which filled over many generations with rainwater and trickling snowmelt. Today, that bowl holds a startlingly blue lake, the deepest in the United States.

Jutting up from the western side of the lake is conical Wizard Island, twinned by the Merriam Cone just below the lake's surface. But hidden geologic features aren't the only surprise contained in Crater Lake's depths. Rainbow trout and kokanee salmon thrive in the otherwise sterile ecology. These fish were introduced between the 1880s and 1940s in a deliberate strategy to attract anglers to the lake. (These days, fishing is still encouraged, but further stocking is verboten.) Visitors may also be lucky enough to spot the "Old Man of the Lake," a thirty-foot tree stump bobbing up and down in the water since at least 1896.

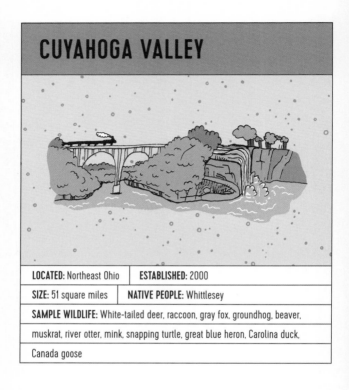

CUYAHOGA VALLEY

LOCATED: Northeast Ohio	**ESTABLISHED:** 2000
SIZE: 51 square miles	**NATIVE PEOPLE:** Whittlesey
SAMPLE WILDLIFE: White-tailed deer, raccoon, gray fox, groundhog, beaver, muskrat, river otter, mink, snapping turtle, great blue heron, Carolina duck, Canada goose	

The gentle mountain streams and secluded trails winding through these valley walls may seem worlds away from anything resembling city life. Yet the Cuyahoga Valley National Park is just a stone's throw outside Cleveland city limits. Set along twenty-two miles of the Cuyahoga River, the park encompasses nearly 33,000 acres of evergreen and deciduous forest in northeastern Ohio. Visitors may begin their journey at the Boston Store, a historic storehouse-turned-visitor center in the heart of the park. Just farther east lie Brandywine Falls, whose misting waters tumble down a sixty-five-foot sandstone gorge. Its current once powered a sawmill at its base. A scenic railroad runs along the river's edge, connecting Akron and Cleveland and stopping at various points throughout the park.

The park was declared a National Recreation Area in 1974, just five years after a fire on the Cuyahoga spurred the restoration of the river's health. The park became Ohio's first, and so far only, national park in 2000.

DEATH VALLEY

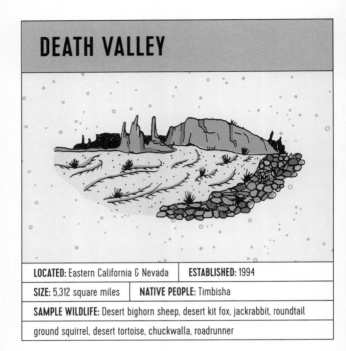

LOCATED: Eastern California & Nevada	ESTABLISHED: 1994
SIZE: 5,312 square miles	NATIVE PEOPLE: Timbisha
SAMPLE WILDLIFE: Desert bighorn sheep, desert kit fox, jackrabbit, roundtail ground squirrel, desert tortoise, chuckwalla, roadrunner	

Given its foreboding name, Death Valley may sound like a wholly inhospitable place. But if you look closely, you'll find the severe desert landscape gives rise to an unexpected bounty of wildlife. The park is home to more than ninety-eight species of animals and 1,000 species of plants, including desert holly, mesquite, and Joshua trees. The hottest temperatures on earth have been recorded here, yet the park contains snow-frosted peaks and wildflower meadows.

Among its many extremes is Badwater Basin, which lies 282 feet below sea level. This fissured salt flat is the lowest point in North America, where the heat seems to rise from the very center of the earth. Be sure to bring plenty of water and sun protection, lest you give added reason for the park's name.

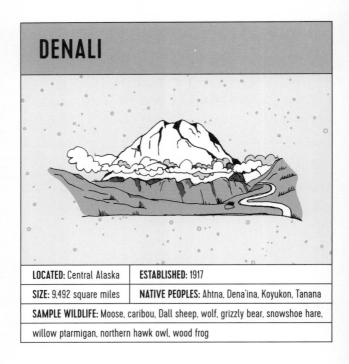

DENALI

LOCATED: Central Alaska	**ESTABLISHED:** 1917
SIZE: 9,492 square miles	**NATIVE PEOPLES:** Ahtna, Dena'ina, Koyukon, Tanana
SAMPLE WILDLIFE: Moose, caribou, Dall sheep, wolf, grizzly bear, snowshoe hare, willow ptarmigan, northern hawk owl, wood frog	

Glaciers drift ever so slowly downslope along the high Alaska Range, trickling their meltwater into great semicircular basins, or "cirques." In this vast and mountainous park, rangers patrol on dogsled, keeping an eye on the caribou, moose, and wolves that call the tundra home. Rising above the snowscape is mighty Denali, the highest peak in all of North America. Past ice ages saw the entire region frozen solid—today, permafrost remains vital in maintaining the health of its boreal ecosystem.

The only road in the park is the mostly gravel Denali Park Road, open to buses, bikes, and those willing to hoof it on foot. The road runs parallel to the Alaska Range, along ninety-two miles of scenic forests and subarctic tundra. Off the beaten path, more than six million acres of open backcountry provide endless opportunity for the willing adventurer. Visitors in the biting winter months may catch a glimpse of the aurora borealis twisting in the sky.

DRY TORTUGAS

LOCATED: Florida Keys	**ESTABLISHED:** 1992
SIZE: 101 square miles	**NATIVE PEOPLE:** ———
SAMPLE WILDLIFE: Green sea turtle, leatherback, masked booby, sooty tern, nurse shark, angelfish, elkhorn coral, staghorn coral	

Lying at the secluded western end of the Florida Keys, Dry Tortugas National Park is the ideal destination for the nautically minded traveler. On Garden Key stands the hexagonal Fort Jefferson, an unfinished naval station built in the early 1800s. Comprised of more than sixteen million bricks, it is considered the largest brick masonry structure in the Western Hemisphere. The *dry* in Dry Tortugas comes from their lack of fresh drinking water, and in order to address this, Fort Jefferson was built with an inventive series of rainwater cisterns in its walls. Today, a daily ferry runs to the structure from Key West, and a campground at the southern end allows visitors to stay overnight on the shore.

Legendary dive sites such as Windjammer and Pulaski Shoals provide the perfect conditions for scuba diving, where coral reefs and seagrass beds support a stunning array of underwater life. The reefy topography of the seabed forms a natural ship trap, which has been the site of 250 wrecks over the centuries. Charter boats offer the chance to dive down and explore these crusted-over relics.

EVERGLADES

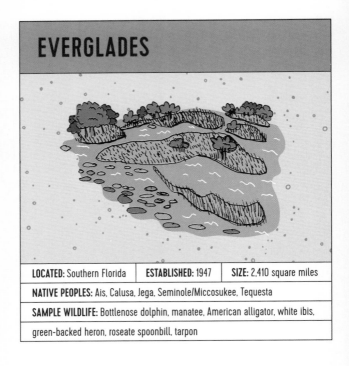

LOCATED: Southern Florida	**ESTABLISHED:** 1947	**SIZE:** 2,410 square miles
NATIVE PEOPLES: Ais, Calusa, Jega, Seminole/Miccosukee, Tequesta		
SAMPLE WILDLIFE: Bottlenose dolphin, manatee, American alligator, white ibis, green-backed heron, roseate spoonbill, tarpon		

Amid the hot and humid sawgrass prairies of South Florida, crisscrossing rivers stretch into the horizon. The elevation here extends no more than a few feet above sea level, with minor shifts (we're talking inches) meaning big changes for the plant and animal life that call the Everglades home. Near the water you might find duckweeds, lemon bacopa, and water lilies, while farther up, lichens grow along the bark of mangrove trees.

The abundance of wildfowl—herons, egrets, spoonbills, cormorants, anhingas, and storks to name a few—make this place a birder's paradise. A few generations ago, the region boasted an even more breathtaking number of skybound creatures. Their populations were severely thinned during a turn-of-the-twentieth-century craze for feathery women's hats. Prevention of the plume trade became a cause célèbre for a fledgling American conservation movement, leading to Pelican Island's establishment as a National Wildlife Refuge.

Today, ongoing threats to the Everglades present new challenges for environmental protection. Early in 2019, a state court permitted an exploratory oil well in the region to move ahead. Rising sea levels and hurricanes threaten to send high levels of salt water into its delicate estuaries and leave the park underwater in a matter of decades. Nevertheless, restoration efforts proceed, bringing back diverse wildlife to the region.

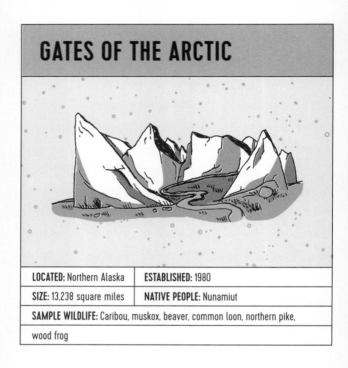

GATES OF THE ARCTIC

LOCATED: Northern Alaska	**ESTABLISHED:** 1980
SIZE: 13,238 square miles	**NATIVE PEOPLE:** Nunamiut
SAMPLE WILDLIFE: Caribou, muskox, beaver, common loon, northern pike, wood frog	

Gates of the Arctic isn't the kind of park where visitors receive a curated experience of guided tours, neatly groomed trails, or cozy amenities. In fact there are no roads, no trails, and no visitor services to speak of within its borders. Its eastern edge starts just five miles from Dalton Highway and is accessible by foot via the village of Anaktuvuk Pass. However, the more common

THIS IS A BOOK FOR PEOPLE WHO LOVE THE NATIONAL PARKS

method of entry is by charter flight. While entry is free (there's hardly anyone to enforce an admissions fee if they tried), the trip out is decidedly costly. The park generally attracts just around ten thousand visitors per year.

Each year, massive caribou herds trek in long caravans across the central Brooks Range. And each year for thousands of years, the nomadic Nunamiut people have trailed these herds on a seasonal hunt. This time-honored ritual is protected within the park, which does not put constraints on native subsistence living. In this way, the park preserves human tradition, as well as the broader ecology.

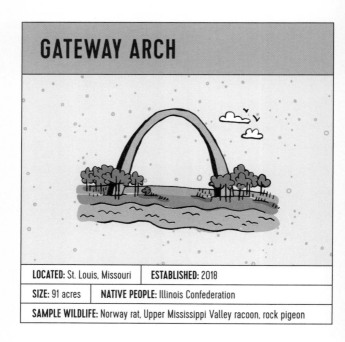

GATEWAY ARCH

LOCATED: St. Louis, Missouri	ESTABLISHED: 2018	
SIZE: 91 acres	NATIVE PEOPLE: Illinois Confederation	
SAMPLE WILDLIFE: Norway rat, Upper Mississippi Valley racoon, rock pigeon		

The lands surrounding St. Louis, Missouri, were once home to the Mississippian culture, a mound-building people known for their architectural marvels. Across the river from the grassy remnants of Cahokia, their largest city, stands a present-day marvel of architecture—the 630-foot stainless-steel span of the tallest arch on earth. The swooping form, designed by architect Eero Saarinen, was built as a tribute to westward expansion, the settler movement that robbed much of North America's native population of their lands. (Many of those lands became the national parks found in this book—see page 4) The archway's status as a national park points to an irony at the heart of the parks movement: that the effort to protect natural, "unpeopled" lands began after a good many people were dispossessed of them. It's a history that deserves large, sweeping reminders.

GLACIER

LOCATED: Northern Montana	ESTABLISHED: 1910
SIZE: 1,583 square miles	NATIVE PEOPLE: Blackfeet, Cree, Gros Ventre,
Kootenai, Salish, Stoneys	
SAMPLE WILDLIFE: Grizzly bear, mountain goat, wolverine, Canada lynx, little	
brown bat, painted turtle, golden eagle, Clark's nutcracker, black swift, lake trout	

This stunningly diverse mountain park preserves one of the oldest intact temperate ecosystems on earth. Despite the timeless beauty of its old-growth forests—full of aspen, cedar, hemlock, and pine—its eponymous glaciers are fast disappearing. Grinnell Glacier, in the heart of the park, can be reached after a six-mile hike (one-way) around the growing proglacial lake at its base. Current trends suggest the park's glaciers will be gone by 2030.

On the scenic Going-to-the-Sun Road, spring snow-melt cascades down onto a narrow two-lane highway, while magnificent views stretch beyond unguarded hairpin turns. Secluded areas such as North Fork and Goat Haunt provide chances to kiss your connectivity goodbye and fully immerse yourself in the natural beauty. Parts of Goat Haunt traverse the U.S.–Canada border, which cuts a treeless scar across the landscape.

GLACIER BAY

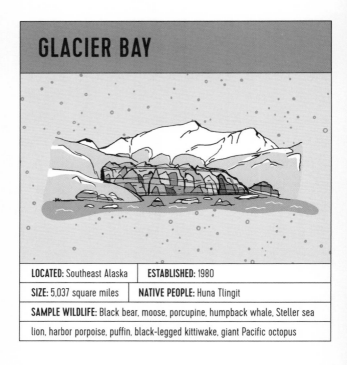

LOCATED: Southeast Alaska	ESTABLISHED: 1980
SIZE: 5,037 square miles	NATIVE PEOPLE: Huna Tlingit
SAMPLE WILDLIFE: Black bear, moose, porcupine, humpback whale, Steller sea lion, harbor porpoise, puffin, black-legged kittiwake, giant Pacific octopus	

Two centuries ago, Glacier Bay was covered in a solid sheet of ice. In its sixty-five-mile retreat, the glacial ice has left a wide-open coastal landscape slowly being claimed by plant and animal life. Seven jagged glaciers spill into the bay, which calve icebergs into the open waters. It's a popular destination for kayaks as well as cruise ships, which are nonetheless dwarfed by the scale of the massive ice wall. Humpback whales can be seen leaping up from beneath the silvery waters, before slapping their large fins on the surface—a practice known as "breaching."

For the 10 percent of visitors who step off the boat, much of the parks' wonders are to be found on land. The nearby town of Gustavus provides the perfect entry point to the park, from which visitors can receive backcountry permits, explore the handful of developed trails in the area, or simply mingle with the locals.

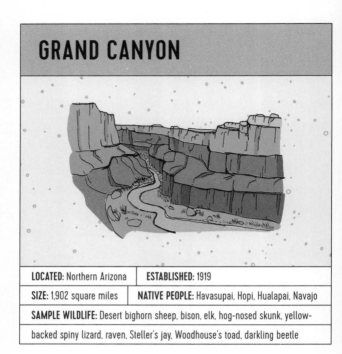

GRAND CANYON

LOCATED: Northern Arizona	**ESTABLISHED:** 1919
SIZE: 1,902 square miles	**NATIVE PEOPLE:** Havasupai, Hopi, Hualapai, Navajo
SAMPLE WILDLIFE: Desert bighorn sheep, bison, elk, hog-nosed skunk, yellow-backed spiny lizard, raven, Steller's jay, Woodhouse's toad, darkling beetle	

The postcards, license plates, novelty key chains, hats, T-shirts, and travel mugs hardly do the Grand Canyon justice. Its staggering vistas have commanded human fascination for centuries. The sedimentary buttes and mesas—in searing reds, subtle pinks and violets, earthen buffs, browns, greens, and grays—seem to stand frozen in time. At this majestic canyon's widest

THIS IS A BOOK FOR PEOPLE WHO LOVE THE NATIONAL PARKS

points, the North and South Rims lie a full eighteen miles apart. Getting from one side to another can take hours without a star-spangled motorcycle to make the leap—like Robbie Knievel in 1999.

Down the Grand Canyon's iconic, rugged slopes, the fossils of mollusks, ferns, and animal tracks are imprinted in the desert stone. Peering up from banks of the Colorado River is as much a showstopper as looking down and just as likely to evade description.

GRAND TETON

LOCATED: Northwestern Wyoming		ESTABLISHED: 1929
SIZE: 485 square miles	NATIVE PEOPLE: Bannock, Blackfeet, Crow, Flathead,	
Gros Ventre, Nez Perce, Shoshone		
SAMPLE WILDLIFE: Moose, buffalo, pronghorn, eagle, trumpeter swan		

Built by tectonic subduction and carved away by thousands of years of glacial activity, the mighty Grand Teton stretches over a mile above the neighboring valley. On calm summer mornings, its jagged peak is perfectly twinned in the surface of Jackson Lake. It is the largest and most impressive peak in the Teton Range, long regarded as a mecca for mountaineers. Though its summit is only accessible to the most experienced climbers, the surrounding peaks, foothills, and valleys of Grand Teton National Park offer something for everyone to enjoy.

The shores of alpine lakes provide the ideal spots for picnicking, wildlife viewing, or pushing off on a morning paddle. Contrary to its name, Lake Solitude is a popular destination for hikers, set at the end of a scenic trail through wildflower meadows along the Cascade Creek. Fellow hikers aren't the only intelligent creatures you'll run into. Moose—stately, majestic, and clumsy-looking all at once—frequently browse here.

GREAT BASIN

LOCATED: Eastern Nevada	ESTABLISHED: 1986
SIZE: 121 square miles	NATIVE PEOPLE: Fremont, Goshute, Paiute, Ute,
Washoe, Western Shoshone	
SAMPLE WILDLIFE: Mule deer, pronghorn, black-tailed jackrabbit, pack rat,	
kilideer, long-billed curlew, golden eagle, Bonneville cutthroat trout	

Past the remote desert valleys and ghost towns along U.S. Route 50 ("The Loneliest Road in America"), this dry and mountainous region is a refuge of high-desert wildlife, including rare groves of ancient bristlecone pines. The oldest known specimen, was found to be more than 5,000 years old. Chief among the park's natural attractions are the Lehman Caves, full of dazzling limestone formations and unusual cave life.

After dark, the low light pollution, low humidity, and high elevation of this park conspire to put on a magnificent show of stars, star clusters, meteors, and satellites, all observable with the naked eye. From the overlook on Wheeler Peak, the Milky Way cuts a wide arc over the sage-covered foothills below.

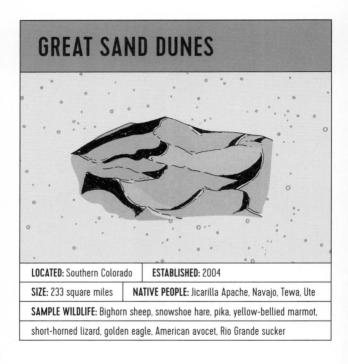

GREAT SAND DUNES

LOCATED: Southern Colorado	**ESTABLISHED:** 2004
SIZE: 233 square miles	**NATIVE PEOPLE:** Jicarilla Apache, Navajo, Tewa, Ute
SAMPLE WILDLIFE: Bighorn sheep, snowshoe hare, pika, yellow-bellied marmot, short-horned lizard, golden eagle, American avocet, Rio Grande sucker	

The southern Colorado wilderness between the Sangre de Cristo and San Juan Mountains plays host to diverse ecologies of wetlands, conifer and aspen forests, alpine lakes, and tundra. But the pièce de résistance of Great Sand Dunes National Park is the thirty-odd square miles of twisting dunes, seemingly miraculously air-dropped from the Sahara. The dunes are the windswept remains of ancient lakes, long since drained from the San Luis Valley. At its highest points, the dazzling sandscape rises to nearly 750 feet.

Visitors must cross the wide but shallow Medano Creek in the spring and summer to reach the golden giants after which this park is named. Once there, hiking up loose, sloping sand can be quite the calf burner. And with summer sand surface temperatures potentially rising to 150°F, it's wise to bring lots of water. Sledding and sandboarding are year-round activities, with gear available to rent throughout the San Luis Valley.

GREAT SMOKY MOUNTAINS

LOCATED: Tennessee–North Carolina border		ESTABLISHED: 1934
SIZE: 816 square miles	NATIVE PEOPLE: Cherokee	
SAMPLE WILDLIFE: Black bear, elk, river otter, tricolored bat, peregrine falcon, downy woodpecker, brook trout, lungless salamander		

A billowy haze rises over Appalachia, as if the fires of creation still burned beneath this peaceful mountain terrain. The fog is a recurring feature, caused by the diverse plant life releasing vaporous organic compounds into the air.

Beneath the sighing treetops, the mysterious old-growth forest hides a rich cultural history. The park encloses part of the historic homeland of the Cherokee Nation, who were chased from the area in 1838. Many residents in the nearby Qualla reservation descend from the fortunate few who hid in the dense forest to evade removal. Also present are traces of Southern Appalachian Mountain culture, a mix of English, Scotch-Irish, and Irish settler communities. The cultures of both these people remain, ever-evolving with their descendants.

Year-round wildflower blooms earn the park a reputation as "Wildflower National Park," with dogwood, flame azalea, mountain laurel, and rhododendron adding brilliant hues to the understory. The park is also home to synchronous fireflies (*Photinus carolinus*), the only species of fireflies in the United States with the ability to flash their lights all together at once. The mating season when this occurs lasts about two weeks, peaking in late May or June.

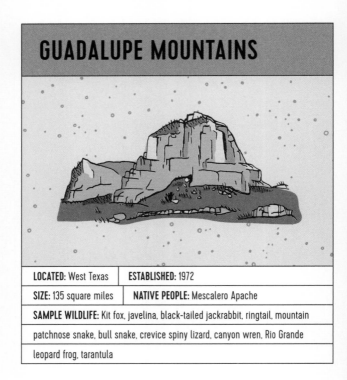

GUADALUPE MOUNTAINS

LOCATED: West Texas	**ESTABLISHED:** 1972
SIZE: 135 square miles	**NATIVE PEOPLE:** Mescalero Apache

SAMPLE WILDLIFE: Kit fox, javelina, black-tailed jackrabbit, ringtail, mountain patchnose snake, bull snake, crevice spiny lizard, canyon wren, Rio Grande leopard frog, tarantula

Rising up from the sunbaked Chihuahuan Desert, the Guadalupe Mountains cut a rugged swath across the horizon. Throughout the Capitan limestone are fossils of spindly, spiraling creatures from the Permian period (roughly 299 million years ago), when this place contained the reefy shallows of a great inland sea. Tens of millions of years later, the Guadalupe Mountains thrust up from the earth's surface, creating the many caves and alcoves that mark the region. Archaeologists have dated pottery, baskets, and projectile points in these caves to over 10,000 years ago.

Guadalupe Peak is the highest point in the state of Texas, its cliffs climbing straight up to an astonishing 8,749 feet. Hikers can choose to summit from the Guadalupe Peak Trail or continue on to its mighty neighbor El Capitan (not to be confused with its namesake in Yosemite). Another popular hiking route is the McKittrick Canyon Trail, which winds between the towering canyon walls. The lush band of greenery is supported by the park's only year-round stream.

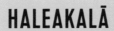

HALEAKALĀ

LOCATED: East Maui	ESTABLISHED: 1961
SIZE: 52 square miles	NATIVE PEOPLE: Native Hawaiian
SAMPLE WILDLIFE: Hawaiian monk seal, ʻopeʻapeʻa (Hawaiian hoary bat), green sea turtle, ʻuaʻu (Hawaiian petrel), nēnē (Hawaiian goose)	

The crumbly sides of this volcanic crater slope down into a lunar-like valley, dotted with over a dozen multicolored cinder cones. Daybreak is the time to come to this sacred "House of the Sun." As the island of Maui awakens, the landscape blazes in radiant hues.

Elsewhere in the park lies the verdant Kīpahulu Valley. The district is a living example of an *ahupuaʻa*, or traditional land division set up to protect natural resources. In this lush ecosystem of streams, rain forests, and bogs, lucky bird-watchers might spot the nene, Hawaii's state bird and a descendant of Canada geese that came to the islands roughly half a million years ago. Before restoration efforts helped the nene's numbers bounce back, there were only thirty left. Today there are estimated to be nearly 3,000 in the wild.

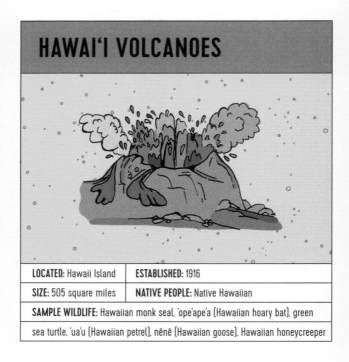

HAWAI'I VOLCANOES

LOCATED: Hawaii Island	ESTABLISHED: 1916
SIZE: 505 square miles	NATIVE PEOPLE: Native Hawaiian
SAMPLE WILDLIFE: Hawaiian monk seal, 'ope'ape'a (Hawaiian hoary bat), green sea turtle, 'ua'u (Hawaiian petrel), nēnē (Hawaiian goose), Hawaiian honeycreeper	

To view the steam vents, lava flows, and pit craters of Hawai'i Volcanoes National Park is to be reminded of a powerful truth: the earth is still being born. The park preserves the landscape around Mauna Loa, the world's most massive shield volcano, and Kīlauea, one of the world's most active volcanoes. Together these two powerful volcanoes have formed and reformed the island of Hawaii for hundreds of thousands of years.

Five-hundred-year-old petroglyphs are carved into the lava surfaces, capturing the lives and beliefs of the ancestral Hawaiian people. Six miles west of the Kīlauea crater, the footprints of an ill-fated warrior party are imprinted in the ash of a 1790 eruption. For generations, people of the island would measure their lives around such events.

Kīlauea had been erupting nearly continuously since 1983, when, in 2018, an explosive blast in the Halema'uma'u Crater sent volcanic ash 30,000 feet into the air. The Kīlauea section of the park remained closed as the lava flow swallowed roadways and houses and even boiled away Hawaii's largest natural freshwater lake. After roughly five months of activity, the eruption was finally declared over. Many park operations have resumed, with the landscape slightly transformed.

HOT SPRINGS

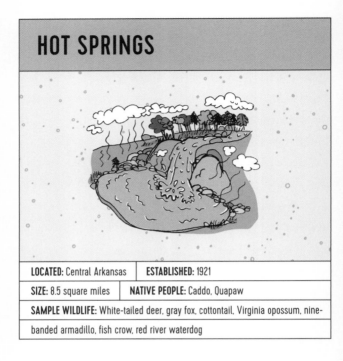

LOCATED: Central Arkansas	ESTABLISHED: 1921
SIZE: 8.5 square miles	NATIVE PEOPLE: Caddo, Quapaw
SAMPLE WILDLIFE: White-tailed deer, gray fox, cottontail, Virginia opossum, nine-banded armadillo, fish crow, red river waterdog	

A relatively tiny park, Hot Springs is the rare U.S. national park where commercial use of its natural resources occurs. The main attractions at this park are the forty-seven geothermal springs, most heated at around 143°F, which these days sit beneath a series of privately run bathhouses. Their waters have been reputed to clear up all sorts of maladies over the years—from nervous afflictions to tuberculosis to "various diseases of women." Long before settlers arrived, the area was known as the "Valley of the Vapors" and had been enjoyed by Native Americans for thousands of years.

The park includes portions of the surrounding city of Hot Springs, a bustling spa town incorporated in 1879. Walking paths wind through the park, where hikers can view blooming wildflowers and gorgeous scenery. Many of the historic bathhouses have been converted into art galleries, run in part by the National Park Service.

INDIANA DUNES

LOCATED: Northwestern Indiana	ESTABLISHED: 2019
SIZE: 24 square miles	NATIVE PEOPLE: Mahican, Mascouten, Meskwaki,
Miami, Potawatomi, Sauk, Shawnee	
SAMPLE WILDLIFE: White-tailed deer, eastern cottontail, fox squirrel, meadow	
vole, great blue heron, sandpiper, Karner blue butterfly	

Set along fifteen miles of the southern Lake Michigan shoreline, these four gently rolling dune ridges together comprise a one-of-a-kind natural marvel. In this uniquely vegetated ecosystem, you might find arctic bearberry growing beside a prickly pear. The landscape of Indiana Dunes boasts some of the most diverse plant life in all the national parks, whose variation makes up a living record of the dunes' history. The younger dunes are active with all stages of plant succession, from bare sands to grasses and woody shrubs. The older dunes, which date back 8,000 to 12,000 years, support complex and stable oak forests. The shape of the beach is ever-changing, becoming wider in the summer months and shortening with the strong winter winds. Beyond their sandy peaks lie marshy wetlands, grass-filled prairies, and hardwood forests, each a further testament to the park's biodiversity.

ISLE ROYALE

LOCATED: Northwest Lake Superior (Northern Michigan)		ESTABLISHED: 1940
SIZE: 893 square miles	NATIVE PEOPLES: Assiniboin, Cree, Ojibwa	
SAMPLE WILDLIFE: Moose, gray wolf, chatty red squirrel, sandhill crane, lake whitefish, brook trout, yellow perch, trout-perch, walleye		

Sweeping like a brushstroke across the face of Lake Superior, the remote stretch of islands known as Isle Royale is the perfect place to retreat for some wilderness therapy. Home to coves, bays, and inland lakes, the park boasts some of the most remote wilderness in all the Great Lakes region. To get to this secluded park, visitors arrive by a scenic six-hour ferry from Houghton,

Michigan—they must commit to the boat, as there are no roads into or out of the park.

On top of trails winding through deciduous forests and rocky shorelines looking out onto stunning views, the park also bears reminders of past human encounters with the island chain. Flooded copper mines and remnants of Scandinavian fishing communities can be found throughout the park. Off its shores, more than a dozen shipwrecks have made their watery graves.

There is no shortage of opportunities for wildlife viewing in Isle Royale either. The park houses a population of roughly 2,000 moose, who likely found their way here in the early 1900s by—how else?—swimming.

JOSHUA TREE

LOCATED: Southern California	ESTABLISHED: 1994
SIZE: 1,250 square miles	NATIVE PEOPLES: Cahuilla, Chemehuevi (Southern Paiute), Serrano

SAMPLE WILDLIFE: Desert kit fox, bobcat, desert kangaroo rat, yellow-backed spiny lizard, diamondback rattlesnake, red-tailed hawk, American kestrel

Joshua Tree National Park lies at the intersection of two deserts, the Colorado and the Mojave. Despite an annual rainfall of just five inches, its ecology sustains a remarkable mix of hardy desert species. The spiny, spindly tree for which the park is named is a member of the genus *Yucca* and has been used by native people for baskets, sandals, and food. Animals such as the Scott's oriole, desert night lizard, and wood rat make their homes among the tree's iconic branches.

The park itself has earned a reputation as a climber's paradise, with more than 8,000 climbing routes among its towering monzogranite. All over are the remnants of the California gold rush, in the 300-some abandoned mines dotting the landscape. The best preserved is the Lost Horse Mine, which stands as a kind of Ozymandian reminder to the folly of human pride and a great way to make your Instagram followers jealous.

KATMAI

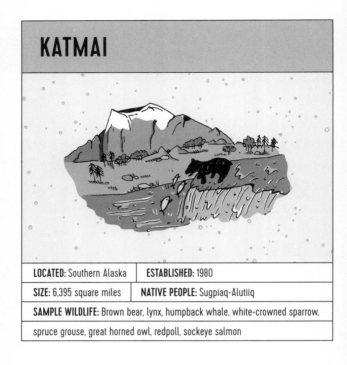

LOCATED: Southern Alaska	ESTABLISHED: 1980
SIZE: 6,395 square miles	NATIVE PEOPLE: Sugpiaq-Alutiiq
SAMPLE WILDLIFE: Brown bear, lynx, humpback whale, white-crowned sparrow, spruce grouse, great horned owl, redpoll, sockeye salmon	

At the inland shoulder of the Alaska Peninsula sits a broad stretch of subarctic wilderness, equal in size to the entire country of Wales. Within this massive park roam its massive inhabitants, the Alaska Peninsula brown bear. Bear watching is among the park's main attractions. Brownies can be seen snatching their river-borne meals from the top of icy cascades in the late spring and early fall, when the salmon run is at its peak.

Lying at the foot of Novarupta Volcano is the Valley of Ten Thousand Smokes, named for its far-out, post-apocalyptic appearance after a 1912 eruption. The valley floor is now blanketed in ash, at certain places a full 700 feet deep. The mythically named River Lethe cuts a canyon through the valley, exposing the layered strata of its ashen walls.

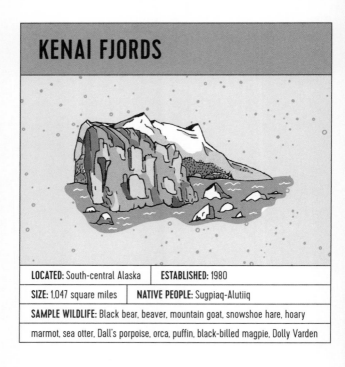

KENAI FJORDS

LOCATED: South-central Alaska	ESTABLISHED: 1980
SIZE: 1,047 square miles	NATIVE PEOPLE: Sugpiaq-Alutiiq

SAMPLE WILDLIFE: Black bear, beaver, mountain goat, snowshoe hare, hoary marmot, sea otter, Dall's porpoise, orca, puffin, black-billed magpie, Dolly Varden

The immense Harding Icefield caps nearly two-thirds of this vast Alaskan park, up to a mile thick in places. Three dozen glaciers spill down from its sides, carving steep and awe-inspiring fjords in the terrain. Exit Glacier is the only part of the park accessible by road, yet it has everything an adventure seeker could be after. Markers along Edge of the Glacier Trail show where the ice has been in recent years, giving a visual indication of its retreat. Hikers in Kenai Fjords can approach the shimmering blue-white face of the frozen behemoth and hear it crackle.

The park's temperate rain forest supports tens of thousands of nesting birds. The surrounding waters provide home to an abundance of marine life, including harbor seals, humpback whales, and orcas.

KINGS CANYON

LOCATED: Sierra Nevada (East-central California)		ESTABLISHED: 1940
SIZE: 722 square miles	NATIVE PEOPLE: Mono, Yokut	
SAMPLE WILDLIFE: Sierra Nevada bighorn sheep, black bear, coyote, lodgepole chipmunk, California quail, northern goshawk, mountain yellow-legged frog		

This rugged granite valley is the work of ancient glaciers, which came in freezes and thaws over the past
2.5 million years. Their journeys carved the mile-deep
walls of King's Canyon, some of the steepest reliefs in
all of North America. At their base lie gently rolling
meadows and streams. The bare peaks of the Great
Western Divide cut through the lower portion of this

park in east-central California, and form a partial border with Sequoia National Park to the south.

Like its sister park, Kings Canyon is a sanctuary of wild *Sequoiadendron giganteum*. The secluded Redwood Mountain Grove is home to over 15,000 sequoias (mistakenly called "redwoods" by early pioneers), the largest concentration anywhere on earth. These specimens were spared from logging, while many in the Converse Basin just a dozen miles north were not so fortunate.

A short walk off the Kings River sits Muir Rock, named for the naturalist who once issued stirring lectures from its level peak. His writing and speechifying—which have the power to inspire to this day—helped bring attention to the significance of the sequoia groves and preserve them from further logging. It sits above a crystal clear swimming hole, the perfect spot to jump in when the waters are calm.

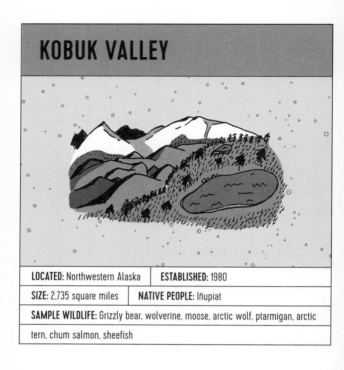

KOBUK VALLEY

LOCATED: Northwestern Alaska	ESTABLISHED: 1980
SIZE: 2,735 square miles	NATIVE PEOPLE: Iñupiat
SAMPLE WILDLIFE: Grizzly bear, wolverine, moose, arctic wolf, ptarmigan, arctic tern, chum salmon, sheefish	

Kobuk Valley is the smaller—yet still decidedly massive—sister park to nearby Gates of the Arctic and is even more difficult to reach. Most famously, the park is home to a bizarre site—hundred-foot-high sand dunes, lying thirty-five miles north of the Arctic Circle. The existence of the Great Kobuk Sand Dunes can be attributed to the last Ice Age, when the ebb and flow of massive ice sheets ground the underlying rocks into a fine sand. Winds collected the sands at the base of a great valley, and by the time the ice retreated, 200,000 acres of magnificent dunes were left behind. Today, most of that territory has been reclaimed by the forest, leaving 16,000 acres still mostly bare. The roots of numerous grasses, sedges, and a native plant called Kobuk locoweed have found purchase in the sand and serve to stabilize the dunes from erosion. These plants further encourage a succession of mosses, lichen, shrubs, and finally, trees. Caribou make their annual migration across the valley's golden peaks, leaving footprints that can be seen all throughout spring and fall.

LAKE CLARK

LOCATED: Southwest Alaska	**ESTABLISHED:** 1980
SIZE: 4,093 square miles	**NATIVE PEOPLE:** Dena'ina, Sugpiaq, Yup'ik
SAMPLE WILDLIFE: Caribou, moose, Dall sheep, red fox, common merganser,	
black-legged kittiwake, golden-crowned sparrow, red-throated loon,	
sockeye salmon	

Bright crimson sockeye salmon wiggle their way up the Newhalen River by the hundreds of thousands, before spilling into the open waters of Lake Clark. The lake runs forty-three miles along scenic Alaskan terrain, enclosed by mountains on all sides. These are the waters where the sockeye are born and, after a few years spent in the open ocean, where they return to spawn. Upon hatching, their young will embark upon the same age-old journey: from lake to sea to lake again.

Here in this park the Alaska and Aleutian ranges converge to create the Chigmit Mountains. Between the sloping tundras, soaring peaks, and icy glaciers, the park features a veritable "best of" what the Alaskan wilderness has to offer. Yet due to its inaccessibility, fewer than 15,000 humans make the trek each year.

LASSEN VOLCANIC

LOCATED: Northern California	ESTABLISHED: 1916
SIZE: 166 square miles	NATIVE PEOPLE: Atsugewi, Maidu, Yahi, Yana
SAMPLE WILDLIFE: Sierra Nevada red fox, bobcat, coyote, mule deer, skunk,	
bufflehead duck, mountain chickadee, long-toed salamander	

This ashen park was created in 1916 to protect the freshly spewed landscape formed by the Lassen Peak volcano. A series of on-and-off eruptions had left behind an alien terrain of boiling mud pots, steaming hot springs, billowing fumaroles, gnarly sulfur vents, multihued cinder cones, and crater lakes. While the 2,000-foot giant has settled down for now, it remains an active volcano and the largest plug-dome volcano in the world. The surrounding conifer forest—of ponderosa pine, white fir, and gooseberry bushes—provides a tranquil counterpoint to the smoldering badlands and goes to show it's not all gloom and doom in this high rocky terrain.

The park doesn't enjoy the name recognition of its closest neighbors, and as such, it boasts modest crowds even in its peak season. Yet its enthralling sights make it well worth a spot on your bucket list.

MAMMOTH CAVE

LOCATED: Central Kentucky	**ESTABLISHED:** 1941
SIZE: 83 square miles	**NATIVE PEOPLE:** Archaic
SAMPLE WILDLIFE: Indiana bat, pygmy shrew, snapping turtle, northern ringneck snake, Kentucky cave shrimp, eyeless cave fish	

Within the limestone maze of Mammoth Cave National Park lies a history as deep and enthralling as the cave itself. Through the mouth of the Historic Entrance, archaeologists have found woven cloth moccasins, pottery, and mining tools, as well as some well-preserved human remains. Most appear to have been intentionally buried, yet one body, nicknamed "Lost John," had been crushed by a boulder while digging for minerals. The earliest commercial tours of the site were led by African American slaves in the nineteenth century. These guides were also explorers, uncovering many parts of the cave still accessed today. They are celebrated as legends, whose stories have become central to park lore.

These days, visitors can opt for a walk along the caves' electric-lit routes or try either of the popular lamplight tours. Brave types can even trek out on one of the park's physically demanding "wild" tours, along its less developed routes. Get ready to suck in your gut—you might be in for a tight squeeze.

MESA VERDE

LOCATED: Southwest Colorado		**ESTABLISHED:** 1906
SIZE: 81 square miles		**NATIVE PEOPLE:** Ancestral Puebloan
SAMPLE WILDLIFE: Coyote, desert cottontail, gray fox, Mesa Verde night snake, Mexican spotted owl		

Some time around 1300 CE, the 20,000-some people of the Green Mesa vacated their carefully laid stone villages and set off for an uncertain fate. In the generations prior, they had enjoyed a peaceable agrarian existence and developed a remarkable form of basketry dating back more than a millennium. In their sudden departure, they left cookware, tools, and clothing.

The archaeological record tells the story: a lifetime of below-average rainfall, dwindling crops, and the violent infighting that ensued. In their trek through the desert, these people either found haven among the Ancestral Puebloans they called neighbors or suffered fatal hardship along the way.

In its present state, Mesa Verde is the only U.S. national park (not historic site) set aside specifically for its historical significance. The story of the Mesa Verdean society can be traced by the presence of three kinds of dwellings—pit house, pueblo, and cliff dwelling. Visitors can observe all three with the careful supervision of a park ranger. The national parks movement could not have come soon enough to this delicate site, which had been the target of careless "curio seekers" before being put under federal protection. Today, it is one of the best-preserved archaeological sites of Ancestral Puebloan culture in the United States.

MOUNT RAINIER

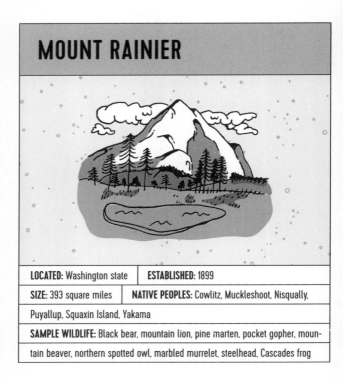

LOCATED: Washington state	ESTABLISHED: 1899	
SIZE: 393 square miles	NATIVE PEOPLES: Cowlitz, Muckleshoot, Nisqually,	
Puyallup, Squaxin Island, Yakama		
SAMPLE WILDLIFE: Black bear, mountain lion, pine marten, pocket gopher, moun-		
tain beaver, northern spotted owl, marbled murrelet, steelhead, Cascades frog		

The glacier-capped peak of Tahoma (commonly re-
ferred to as Mount Rainier) towers a full 14,410 feet
above sea level, making it the fourth-highest mountain in the contiguous United States. It also happens
to be one of the most dangerous active volcanoes on
earth. For the time being, however, Mount Rainier is a

tranquil spot for all kinds of outdoor activities, including hiking, camping, and wildlife viewing.

In the spring, the subalpine meadows come alive, and the foot of the mountain teems with blues, purples, greens, reds, and whites. These wildflowers are acutely responsive to the turning seasons, making them excellent gauges of the effects of climate change on the area. Through a program called "MeadoWatch," visitors are invited to become citizen scientists and share their wildflower photos with researchers at the University of Washington.

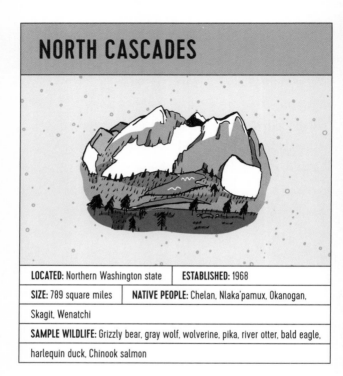

NORTH CASCADES

LOCATED: Northern Washington state		ESTABLISHED: 1968
SIZE: 789 square miles	NATIVE PEOPLE: Chelan, Nlaka'pamux, Okanogan,	
Skagit, Wenatchi		
SAMPLE WILDLIFE: Grizzly bear, gray wolf, wolverine, pika, river otter, bald eagle,		
harlequin duck, Chinook salmon		

This rugged alpine region encompasses the remotest territory in the Pacific Northwest. The park contains only one unpaved road, no human settlements, and few overnight campgrounds.

In recent years, the park's 300 glaciers have dwindled and traces of wind-borne pollutants have been detected in the air and water. Yet one threat to the alpine ecosystem may be easily overlooked—or rather, over-heard. The North Cascades Natural Sounds Program works to preserve the park's *acoustic* resources—the whistling marmot calls, thundering rockfalls, and dawn choruses of birds that echo in the clear mountain air. By placing digital recording devices throughout the park, scientists check up on the state of the region's delicate soundscape, keeping an ear out for noise pollution. Visitors are encouraged to "tread lightly and speak softly," in order to leave the park truly undisturbed.

OLYMPIC

LOCATED: Northern Washington state	ESTABLISHED: 1938
SIZE: 1,442 square miles	NATIVE PEOPLE: Hoh, Jamestown S'Klallam, Lower
Elwha Klallam, Makah, Port Gamble, Quileute, Quinault, S'Klallam, Skokomish	
SAMPLE WILDLIFE: Gray whale, Olympic marmot, Olympic snow mole, northern	
spotted owl, rhinoceros auklet, sockeye salmon, Olympic torrent salamander	

A thick mat of moss carpets the forest floor of Olympic National Park. It also hangs down from the branches of ancient spruces and hemlocks. Sound has nowhere to go in this rare temperate zone rain forest, its cushiony green surfaces submerging the air in a dense silence. The roots of growing trees struggle to find purchase in this mossy floor—instead, new growth rises up from old stumps and hollow logs.

From a cluster of snowcapped mountains at the heart of the park, crystal clear snowmelt runs down through gently sloping river valleys. Timberline lies low on these slopes; above it, many-hued alpine meadows can be found.

Along seventy-three miles of Pacific coastline, diverse stretches of beach—some rocky, some sandy—extend into the calmly lapping waves. Just three miles inland lies the freshwater Ozette Lake. From its shore, a boardwalk trail leads through a boggy wood of western red cedar, licorice ferns, and salal.

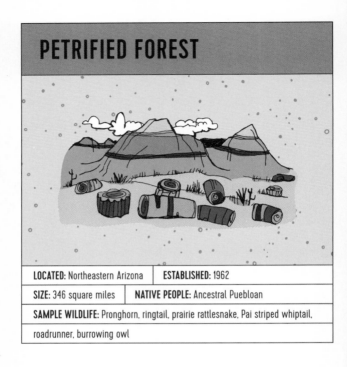

PETRIFIED FOREST

LOCATED: Northeastern Arizona	ESTABLISHED: 1962
SIZE: 346 square miles	NATIVE PEOPLE: Ancestral Puebloan
SAMPLE WILDLIFE: Pronghorn, ringtail, prairie rattlesnake, Pai striped whiptail, roadrunner, burrowing owl	

Step into a stony graveyard of trees, as astonishing in death as they had been in life. These massive conifers were alive a full 225 million years ago, in the Late Triassic period. In those days, Northern Arizona was a flat subtropical expanse on the continent of Pangaea, right by the equator. Gradually, the trees were swept up and carried downriver, then buried in volcanic sediment. Their porous wood absorbed minerals over time, replacing their internal structures with solid quartz. Now they poke out from the eroded clay hills and cliff faces, glimmering red, orange, yellow, and purple in the Arizona sun. Echoing the kaleidoscope appearance of the stumps are the colorful mineral layers of the Painted Desert, formed by many of the same geologic forces.

Traces of Ancestral Puebloan life are scattered throughout the park, including the partially restored Agate House. The eight-room pueblo was constructed between seven hundred and nearly a thousand years ago out of the area's abundant supply of—you guessed it—petrified wood.

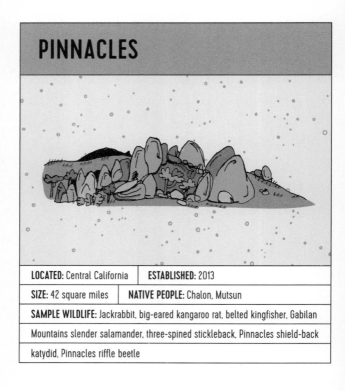

PINNACLES

LOCATED: Central California	ESTABLISHED: 2013
SIZE: 42 square miles	NATIVE PEOPLE: Chalon, Mutsun
SAMPLE WILDLIFE: Jackrabbit, big-eared kangaroo rat, belted kingfisher, Gabilan Mountains slender salamander, three-spined stickleback, Pinnacles shield-back katydid, Pinnacles riffle beetle	

Low-lying chaparral shrubs sweep across these California hills set within the San Andreas Fault Zone in the central part of the state. The dry brushlands—of greasewood, manzanita, and gray pine—creep up bare volcanic rock, from which the smooth tapering Pinnacles rise.

Down below lie the park's famous talus caves, formed by tumbling boulders which came to rest between the canyon walls. Local legend claims the bandit Tiburcio Vásquez took shelter in these caves and tucked away a treasure deep inside. These days, Balconies Cave Trail offers an unguided, unlit scramble through the ghostly corridor. Headlamps are encouraged, as are some extra batteries.

A compacted dirt trail through High Peaks snakes across narrow cliff faces, switchbacks, and thigh-burning terrain. The critically endangered California condor soars overhead, at times giving hikers the sense they're being watched.

REDWOOD

LOCATED: Northern California coast	**ESTABLISHED:** 1968
SIZE: 206 square miles	**NATIVE PEOPLE:** Hupa, Karuk, Tolowa, Yurok

SAMPLE WILDLIFE: Roosevelt elk, California sea lion, bald eagle, giant green anemone, banana slug

Enter ancient stands of the world's tallest living trees, soaring upward of 300 feet into the California sky. Some of these stately giants were saplings way back in the days of Confucius, 2,500 years ago. High above the forest floor, their limbs develop deep organic soil mats, from which grow different species of plants, shrubs, and even other full-size trees! Entire ecosystems live 150 feet above the forest floor of Redwood National Park.

This once-sprawling forest is thought to have covered two million acres but was diminished by logging well into the twentieth century. In 1978, Congress expanded the park by nearly 90 percent of its original size, including entire hillsides that had been rendered graveyards by clear-cutting. The replanted redwoods are expected to grow to a modest size in another 250 years. Careful monitoring ensures that they can mature in conditions as close as possible to their ideal natural state.

Along a foggy stretch of California coast, visitors might step into placid tide pools to carefully uncover sea stars and hermit crabs. In virtually all the park's habitats—forests, prairies, streams, and marshes—the hulking Roosevelt elk can be observed.

ROCKY MOUNTAIN

LOCATED: Northern Colorado	**ESTABLISHED:** 1915

SIZE: 414 square miles, with 395 square miles of adjoining U.S. Forest Service lands

NATIVE PEOPLES: Arapaho, Cheyenne, Comanche, Ute

SAMPLE WILDLIFE: Beaver, bighorn sheep, snowshoe hare, mountain lion, moose, mountain chickadee, white-tailed ptarmigan, cutthroat trout

Lush meadows and glades yield to high snow-mantled tundra in this iconic alpine park. Human presence among its soaring peaks dates all the way back to the Paleoindians who hunted and foraged along the present-day Trail Ridge Road. For generations, families availed themselves of the elk and mountain sheep and cultivated edible plants such as blueberries and alpine spring beauty. They were followed by the Ute and Arapaho, who migrated between high- and lowlands over centuries. By the early 1860s, the Arapaho had made their latest retreat from the high country, just a few years before U.S. troops swept through Colorado Territory with literal guns blazing.

A half-century later, the national parks movement was at its peak, and plans for a federally protected park in the Rockies were coming together. Members of the Colorado Mountain Club consulted two Arapaho elders, Gun Griswold and Sherman Sage, to ride through the park's soon-to-exist borders and name the many features they recalled from their youth. These names, such as Neota Creek and Niwot Ridge, are in common use to this day.

SAGUARO

LOCATED: Southern Arizona	ESTABLISHED: 1994
SIZE: 143 square miles	NATIVE PEOPLE: Akimel O'odham, Apache, Hopi,
Maricopa, Tohono O'odham, Yaqui, Yavapai, Zuni	
SAMPLE WILDLIFE: Bobcat, javelina, desert tortoise, Gila monster, roadrunner,	
vermilion flycatcher, whiskered screech owl, leopard frog	

Saguaro is named for the iconic cactus scattered throughout the Sonoran Desert and concentrated throughout these twin Arizona parks. The desert titans can grow up to sixty feet tall and thrive in scorching conditions for up to 200 years. Their accordion-like pleated trunks allow the saguaros to store nearly a ton of water and expand as they grow fat in the rainy season. Plump red fruits burst from their crowns, a favorite of birds, harvester ants, and desert mammals such as the javelina and ground squirrel.

Eight hundred years ago, members of the Hohokam culture lived among these giants and made etchings in the desert sandstone. Their sacred works can still be seen today on a brief hike through the Tuscon Mountain District of the park.

SEQUOIA

LOCATED: Sierra Nevada (East-central California)		**ESTABLISHED:** 1890
SIZE: 631 square miles	**NATIVE PEOPLE:** Foothill Yokut, Tubatulabal, Western	
Mono (Monache)		
SAMPLE WILDLIFE: Black bear, mountain lion, Townsend's big-eared bat, Sierra		
Nevada bighorn sheep, California mountain kingsnake, little kern, golden trout		

If ever you find yourself in need of an ego check, stand next to a giant sequoia for a distinctly humbling experience. Several stories tall, these rare behemoths grow in nature only on the western slopes of the Sierra Nevada. The occasional dose of wildfire helps the trees release seeds from their serotinous cones into the bare mineral soil below. Giant Forest, at the heart of the park, is home of the most massive sequoia specimens. The largest among them, General Sherman, is 275 feet tall, 36 feet in diameter at the base, and 12 million pounds. It is the largest tree on earth by mass.

Among the wildflowers of Huckleberry Meadow Trail sits the former site of Kaweah Colony, a utopian commune begun in the mid-1880s. Its members were forced out thanks to the powerful sway of the Southern Pacific Railroad, which had some help from the U.S. cavalry. A one-room Squatter's Cabin is all that remains.

SHENANDOAH

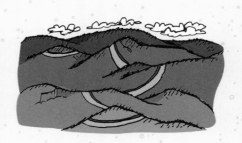

LOCATED: Blue Ridge Mountains (Virginia)	ESTABLISHED: 1935
SIZE: 311 square miles	NATIVE PEOPLES: Catawba, Cherokee, Delaware,
Haudenosaunee, Piedmont Siouan, Shawnee, Susquehannock	
SAMPLE WILDLIFE: Black bear, white-tailed deer, gray squirrel, coyote, Carolina	
chickadee, barred owl, eastern brook trout, Shenandoah salamander	

Sun-dappled oak leaves tumble to the forest floor. The drumming of a woodpecker carries in the midmorning air. Trickling toward the overlooks, campgrounds, and wayside gift shops along Skyline Drive, a caravan of leaf peepers motor past the Rockfish Gap entrance. Autumn has come to the Blue Ridge Mountains.

Shenandoah National Park runs a narrow 105-mile strip over the crest of these Virginia highlands. Human settlement isn't far, with nearby towns providing a scenic complement to the leafy expanse. Since the park's founding, the area has grown over 10 percent more forested, though the chestnuts and northern red oaks are no longer as dominant as they were. Other species such as yellow poplar, maple, basswood, cherry, and birch have carved out their shares of the landscape and added to the diversity of the overstory. While the Shenandoah may seem as old as time, this forest is ever-changing.

THEODORE ROOSEVELT

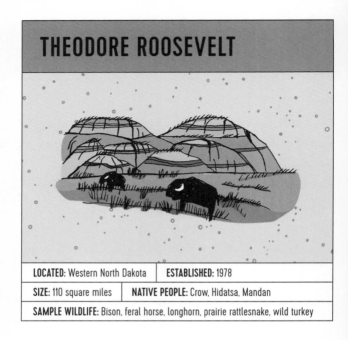

LOCATED: Western North Dakota		**ESTABLISHED:** 1978
SIZE: 110 square miles	**NATIVE PEOPLE:** Crow, Hidatsa, Mandan	
SAMPLE WILDLIFE: Bison, feral horse, longhorn, prairie rattlesnake, wild turkey		

Named for the immortal man who helped kick off the national parks movement, Theodore Roosevelt National Park is a colorful, quiet place where the rush of swaying grass mingles with the babbling of rivers. The seasons seem to bring a mood change to the landscape, with the brown prairie grasses turning a lush green in early summer. The park is split into two sections, threaded by the Little Missouri River. Between them lie sweeping grasses, themselves protected as the Little Missouri National Grassland. Each unit has its own scenic drive, as well as ample spots for hiking, camping, picnicking, canoeing, and wildlife viewing.

Its namesake arrived in the Dakota Territory to hunt bison, which he did, though his time there would inspire his journey toward becoming a conservationist. President Roosevelt's historic Elkhorn Ranch still lies on the western edge of the grasslands, where he would sit on his veranda and read in the shade of cottonwoods.

VIRGIN ISLANDS

LOCATED: The Caribbean	ESTABLISHED: 1956
SIZE: 23 square miles	NATIVE PEOPLE: Ciboney, Igneri, Kalinago, Taino

SAMPLE WILDLIFE: Jamaican fruit bat, spotted dolphin, green iguana, leatherback, red-footed tortoise, bananaquit, Atlantic blue marlin, hammerhead shark, nurse shark, parrotfish, coqui, fire coral

Occupying two-thirds of the island of St. John and more than 5,500 acres of surrounding ocean, Virgin Islands National Park offers a haven for reefs, white sand beaches, and lush tropical fauna. Hike through miles of forest or stop by the twin beaches of Trunk and Cinnamon Bay for a relaxing day on the shore. Campgrounds offer furnished canvas tents and screened cottages along the sand.

Scattered across the island are the relics of early Carib Indian culture and the ruins of the Dutch colonial slave economy. Walkways with educational signage cut through the Annaberg historic district, which features a partially restored sugar plantation.

The hawksbill is one of the only remaining turtle species to regularly nest on the island, though leatherbacks and green sea turtles have been spotted as well. A sea turtle monitoring program relies on volunteers to identify nesting sites and mitigate threats to the nesting females and hatchlings. Visitors are encouraged to notify park rangers if they stumble on a potential nesting site.

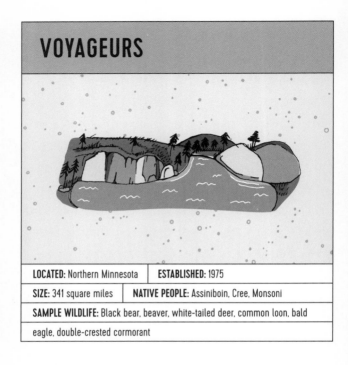

VOYAGEURS

LOCATED: Northern Minnesota		ESTABLISHED: 1975
SIZE: 341 square miles	NATIVE PEOPLE: Assiniboin, Cree, Monsoni	
SAMPLE WILDLIFE: Black bear, beaver, white-tailed deer, common loon, bald eagle, double-crested cormorant		

This watery region was once traversed by canoeing French Canadian fur traders, known as *voyageurs*. Their birch-bark canoes have yielded to the fiberglass and plastic of modern canoes, kayaks, and motorboats, which dot these northern Minnesota lakes throughout the summer. Around 40 percent of the park's area is water, leaving most places accessible only by boat. In the winter, the icy waterways open up opportunities for cross-country skiing, snowmobiling, and snowshoeing. On the Kabetogama Peninsula, wild berries grow in the understory of great spruce, birch, and oak forests.

As night falls, the forest descends into an all-embracing quietude, interspersed with echoing loon calls and the howling of wolves. Overhead, the lucky camper might spot the aurora borealis shimmering above the pines.

WIND CAVE

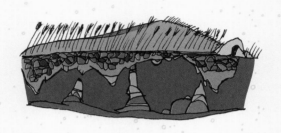

LOCATED: South Dakota	ESTABLISHED: 1903
SIZE: 53 square miles	NATIVE PEOPLE: Cheyenne, Lakota
SAMPLE WILDLIFE: Raccoon, elk, bison, ermine, black-footed ferret, prairie dog, stoat, red-sided garter snake, snapping turtle, poorwill, grosbeak, eastern kingbird	

Set in the Black Hills of South Dakota, this chiefly sub-terranean park protects one of the longest and most intricate cave systems known on earth. The cave is sacred to the Lakota, who trace their origins to the ancestral Buffalo Nation born from its primeval depths. Throughout the cave's 150 miles of mapped passages are rare and remarkable boxwork calcite formations, whose crisscrossing niches resemble a kind of scratchy honeycomb. The cave is named for the eerie "breathing" effect that happens when the air pressure between the mouth of the cave and its inner chambers varies (sudden barometric shifts are common to the western South Dakota weather).

Above ground sits the largest remaining natural mixed-grass prairie in the United States, as well as rolling pine-covered hills and woodland ravines. Wildlife abounds, including scuttling prairie dogs and large, slow-footed bison.

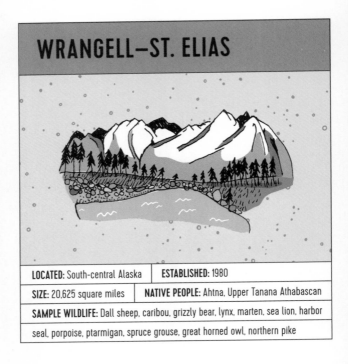

WRANGELL–ST. ELIAS

LOCATED: South-central Alaska	**ESTABLISHED:** 1980
SIZE: 20,625 square miles	**NATIVE PEOPLE:** Ahtna, Upper Tanana Athabascan
SAMPLE WILDLIFE: Dall sheep, caribou, grizzly bear, lynx, marten, sea lion, harbor seal, porpoise, ptarmigan, spruce grouse, great horned owl, northern pike	

What would possibly sum up the most ginormous national park on the North American continent? This massive "mountain kingdom of North America" is larger than seventy of the world's independent countries, lying at the convergence of the Chugach, Wrangell, St. Elias, and Alaska mountain ranges. Its biggest glacier alone exceeds the size of Rhode Island. Among its many ecosystems are spacious tundras, dense snow forests, flat glacial valleys threaded by icy rivers, and cragged alpine peaks. Yet despite its size, the park is not overcrowded with visitors, meaning a hiker could trek many of its unexplored mountains for a lifetime and never see a fellow soul. They just might want to check in with a ranger station from time to time.

YELLOWSTONE

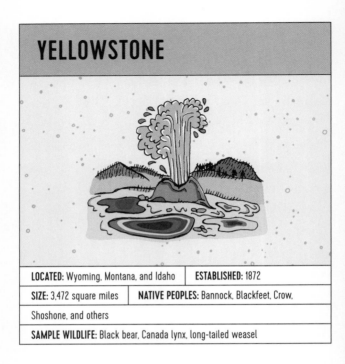

LOCATED: Wyoming, Montana, and Idaho		ESTABLISHED: 1872
SIZE: 3,472 square miles	NATIVE PEOPLES: Bannock, Blackfeet, Crow,	
Shoshone, and others		
SAMPLE WILDLIFE: Black bear, Canada lynx, long-tailed weasel		

"For the benefit and enjoyment of the people" are the words adorning the triumphal entrance at Roosevelt Arch. This is Yellowstone, the world's first national park. Geothermal wonders abound, thanks to the churning hot magma underneath the Yellowstone Caldera. The park boasts more plentiful geysers than anywhere else on earth, spewing magnificent plumes

THIS IS A BOOK FOR PEOPLE WHO LOVE THE NATIONAL PARKS

of all sizes. Boiling mud pots bubble and pop at their base. Fumaroles send up billowing clouds of steam that slip off on the wind.

From the canyon above Yellowstone River, a canopy of lodgepole pine extends to the horizon. Toward higher elevations, whitebark pine, Engelmann spruce, and subalpine fir can also be found. To those who know to look, other more ancient forests reveal themselves—in the petrified stumps tucked away in the northeast corner of the park. Along Specimen Ridge, the fossilized leaves of a dozen different forests peek out from the exposed rock face.

In the windswept grasses of Lamar Valley, sauntering herds of elk and bison graze. The Yellowstone bison herd is the oldest and largest public herd in the United States, with a current count of around 4,500. The sight of them offers just a modest glimpse of what the continent was like, when tens of millions of bison roamed.

YOSEMITE

LOCATED: Sierra Nevada (Northern California)		**ESTABLISHED:** 1890
SIZE: 1,169 square miles	**NATIVE PEOPLES:** Ahwahneechee	
SAMPLE WILDLIFE: American black bear, Sierra Nevada bighorn sheep, mule deer, bobcat, coyote, fisher, acorn woodpecker, Sierra Nevada yellow-legged frog		

Four million people a year make the trip to these sheer granite bluffs, giant sequoia groves, clear mountain streams, and high roaring falls, to experience a bit of what John Muir called the "deep peace of the solemn old woods." This is the landscape that first inspired the national parks idea, where Muir wandered for years before setting off on a life of simple advocacy for the natural world. His example and works are vital to understanding the national parks movement.

One of Muir's greatest losses was the damming of Hetch Hetchy Valley, now under 1,800 feet of water. "Nothing dollarable is safe," he wrote at the time. A smaller dam, the Cascades Diversion Dam, was later constructed just west of Yosemite Valley, before being removed in 2004. The National Park Service now works to restore the Merced River's riparian habitat downriver.

Muir was hardly the first person to care deeply for Yosemite Valley. The Ahwahneechee had been living among its high granite peaks for 3,000 years prior to the young Scot's arrival. Some of the first colonizers to pass through were members of a California state militia, the Mariposa Battalion, who razed and set fire to Ahwahneechee villages. Those who survived the raids struggled to return and were again evicted numerous times over the ensuing decades. These stories of violence and dispossession were repeated throughout many of the present-day parks. They, too, are vital to understanding the national parks movement.

ZION

LOCATED: Southern Utah	ESTABLISHED: 1919
SIZE: 232 square miles	NATIVE PEOPLES: Paiute, Parowan Fremont, Ute,
Virgin Anasazi	
SAMPLE WILDLIFE: Bighorn sheep, mountain lion, mule deer, California condor,	
peregrine falcon	

Water trickles down the steep sandstone walls on either side of the Virgin River, sustaining plants that hang from the joints and cracks of the rock face. The Paiute name for this place is Mukuntuweap, meaning "Straight Canyon." Early Mormon settlers in southern Utah called this majestic landscape "Zion," a promised land after their long journey across the desert from lands further east.

A walk upriver offers plenty of chances to wade in its rocky shallows. True to the name "The Narrows," the gorge running through this tapering slot canyon leaves only a thin band of sky visible to the hikers below. At some spots, the 1,000-foot walls stand a mere twenty feet apart.

Higher up, the Angels Landing hike winds a precarious trail across narrow ridges and drop-off points. Those brave enough to take their eyes off their feet are rewarded with striking views of the park below.

QUICK PARK FACTS

Yellowstone boasts more plentiful geysers than anywhere else on earth, thanks to the volcanic activity underfoot in the Yellowstone Caldera.

The "dry" in "Dry Tortugas" comes from their lack of fresh drinking water. The park's historic Fort Jefferson was built with a series of rainwater cisterns in its walls.

Many of the place-names in Rocky Mountain National Park come from a 1914 expedition by two Arapaho elders, who recalled the natural landmarks of their youth.

The stony stumps and logs of Petrified Forest date back to when the Northern Arizona desert was a flat subtropical plain.

Capitol Reef lies along the Waterpocket Fold, an upthrust crest in the earth extending a hundred miles across the Utah desert.

Carlsbad Caverns was formed by an "acid bath" of groundwater and hydrogen sulfide, which ate away at the underground limestone as the water table descended.

The Paiute name for Zion is Mukuntuweap, meaning "Straight Canyon."

The Kīpahulu District of Haleakalā is an example of an *ahupua'a*, a traditional land division set up to protect natural resources.

A semi-regular dose of wildfires allows the massive sequoia to release its seeds into the soil below.

The Everglades' incredible bird populations were severely thinned during a turn-of-the-20th-century craze for feathered hats.

The namesake cactus of Saguaro National Park often grows between forty and sixty feet tall and can thrive in scorching conditions for up to 200 years.

The Channel Islands have been called "California's Galápagos" for the archipelago's many endemic species. They have sat isolated from the mainland since they were formed.

Acadia's diverse treescape was ensured by the Fire of 1947, which burned many of its old-growth evergreens and gave sun-loving species a chance to thrive.

The inhabitants of Mesa Verde fled around 1300 CE, leaving behind cookware, tools, clothing, and 600 cliff dwellings.

Indiana Dunes enjoys some of the most diverse plant life in all the national parks. You might find Arctic bearberry growing beside prickly pear cactus.

The massive branches of redwood trees accrue deep organic soil mats, from which plants, shrubs, and even other full-size trees can grow.

The Great Smoky Mountains are named for the hazy mist often seen rising from the treetops.

The clear blue Crater Lake is the deepest lake in the United States, formed when Mount Mazama erupted and collapsed 7,700 years ago.

According to Paiute lore, the hoodoos of Bryce Canyon were once the ancient Legend People, who were turned to stone by Coyote for abusing the desert's resources.

Lassen Volcanic National Park was established in 1916 to protect the landscape formed by the newly erupted Lassen Peak volcano.

Wind Cave is named for the eerie "breathing" effect that occurs when the air pressure between the mouth of the cave and its inner chambers varies.

The name Black Canyon of the Gunnison derives from the park's eerie black-stained walls, parts of which receive less than an hour's sunlight in a single day.

Ninety-five percent of Biscayne National Park is underwater.

At a sprawling 20,625 square miles, Alaska's Wrangell—St. Elias is the most massive national park in the United States.

In Olympic National Park's mossy rain forest, new trees can be seen taking root in old stumps and hollow logs.

Big Bend is named for the broad meandering path carved by the Rio Grande through the Chihuahuan Desert.

Arches' Landscape Arch is considered the longest natural stone span in North America.

Voyageurs is named for the French Canadian fur trappers who once paddled birch-bark canoes through the waterways of northern Minnesota.

At their current rate of erosion, the sandstone buttes and pinnacles of Badlands will be around for only 500,000 more years.

ACKNOWLEDGMENTS

A very special thanks to David Garczynski, Shannon Connors Fabricant, Jenna McBride, and the incredible Brainstorm crew. Further gratitude goes out to all those fighting to restore right relations with the natural world: the climate strikers, water protectors, permaculture thinkers, indigenous caretakers, and eco-activists of all ages. This book is especially indebted to the indigenous people of the Turtle Island continent, to whom our "national" parks truly belong.